CW00350512

Rick and Morty

THE WORLD
ACCORDING TO
RICK

Rick Sanchez, as told to Matt Carson

ilex

[adult swim]

An Hachette UK Company
www.hachette.co.uk

First published in Great Britain in 2018
by Ilex Press, an imprint of
Octopus Publishing Group Ltd
Carmelite House
50 Victoria Embankment
London EC4Y 0DZ
www.octopusbooks.co.uk

Published in the US by Hachette Books
Hachette Book Group
1290 Avenue of the Americas
New York, NY 10104

TM & © 2018 Cartoon Network.
Jacket copyright © 2018 by Hachette Book Group, Inc.

All rights reserved. No part of this work may be reproduced or utilized in any
form or by any means, electronic or mechanical, including photocopying,
recording or by any information storage and retrieval system, without the
prior written permission of the publisher.

Publisher: Alison Starling
Licensing Director: Roly Allen
Managing Editor: Rachel Silverlight
Publishing Assistant: Stephanie Hetherington
Senior Production Manager: Peter Hunt

ISBN 978-1-78157-694-6

A CIP catalogue record for this book is available from the British Library

Printed and bound in the Czech Republic

10 9 8 7 6 5 4 3 2 1

Dedication

"I dedicate this book to myself."

— Rick

Introduction

If you've looked at the cover, you're already aware I'm Rick Sanchez. Specifically, Earth C-137 Rick Sanchez. If you know me, you also know I have a grandson named Morty, whom I bring on adventures and BLEEP in assorted galaxies and dimensions and whatnot. I'm never without a sidekick when I have one of the infinite number of Mortys available to me in the multiverse. Unless, of course, I can get it done solo, in which case no sidekick is exactly what I'd prefer. Barring that, Morty it is.

Every Rick needs a Morty, myself included. There are many like him, but this one is mine. If he's gonna be worth a damn in the field, I have to keep him tuned up and in good working order. To take him on adventures, I have to train him to go on adventures, and to train him to go on adventures, I have to take him on adventures. It's like a snake barfing its own tail.

He wastes most of his time at Harry Herpson High School, ostensibly to learn stuff, although it's pointless to bother. School is a cruel trick Earth parents inflict on their young for no other reason than retribution for the deception once inflicted on themselves.

Then there's Summer, the other grandkid. Typically, chicks and adventures have never been a match made in nonexistent heaven for me, but Summer has proven to be an exception.

As to be expected in the Sanchez gene, she's a quick wit and tough cookie, despite her superficial attachments to social media and her phone.

The mother of these two idiots and my beautiful daughter is Beth. Despite her decision to marry Jerry, she is way smarter than she's willing to admit. But if I'm perfectly frank with you, I'm shocked she never drove her car into the ocean with the kids in the trunk. The apple doesn't fall far from the crazy tree.

And Jerry? Ugh, never mind.

But hey, they're family, right? That's gotta mean something, even to the smartest being that's ever existed in the multiverse, aka me, Rick Sanchez. Plus, my lab is set up in their garage, rent-free.

While keeping these dum-dums safe can be a pretty dangerous business, it's nothing compared to the [BLEEP] I've seen. This is why I've decided to share my acquired wisdom with you plebs. As the most intelligent being in the multiverse, I've got a lot of knowledge to drop. Check out this collection of my words of wisdom. If you're smart, you'll pay attention.

Wubba lubba dub dub,
Rick

"I like to shoot straight.
I'm a man of science."

The World According to Rick

"Sometimes science is more
art than science, Morty. A lot
of people don't get that."

Rick on Science and Technology

8

The World According to Rick

"Lemme ask you a question, real quick.
Does evil exist, and if so, can one
detect and measure it?
Rhetorical question. The answer is yes.
You just have to be a genius."

Rick on Science and Technology

"I've certainly seen worse
ionic cell dioxination."

The World According to Rick

"You know the worst part about inventing teleportation? Suddenly you're able to travel the whole galaxy and the first thing you learn is you're the last guy to invent teleportation."

Rick on Science and Technology

322

2
8
18
32
64
64
64
32
16
14
8

Isotope 322

So powerful it makes Isotope 465
look like Isotope 317

189.311

12

"Isotope 322. This stuff's so powerful, Morty, it makes Isotope 465 look like Isotope 317."

Rick on Science and Technology

"I don't do magic, Morty.
I do science. One takes brains,
the other takes dark eyeliner."

The World According to Rick

"I don't respect therapy. Because I'm a scientist. Because I invent, transform, create, and destroy for a living, and when I don't like something about the world, I change it. And I don't think going to a rented office in a strip mall to listen to some agent of averageness explain which words mean which feelings has ever helped anyone do anything. I think it's helped a lot of people get comfortable and stop panicking, which is a state of mind we value in the animals we eat, but not something I want for myself."

The World According to Rick

"I dabble in precision, and if you think you can even approach it with your sad, naked caveman eyeballs, you're the reason this species is a failure."

Rick on Science and Technology

18

The World According to Rick

"So everyone's supposed to sleep every single night now? Do you realize that nighttime makes up half of all time?"

Rick on Space and Time

"Take a good look down there, Morty, and soak it in, because once I pull this lever, it's all back to normal."

The World According to Rick

"Look around you, Morty. Do you
really think this world is real?
You'd have to be an idiot not to
notice all the sloppy details."

Rick on Space and Time

The World According to Rick

"There's pros and cons to every alternate timeline. Fun facts about this one: It's got giant telepathic spiders, eleven nine-elevens, and the best ice cream in the multiverse!"

Rick on Space and Time

"The universe is a crazy, chaotic place."

The World According to Rick

"I try to shelter you from certain realities, Morty, because if I let you make me nervous, then we can't get schwifty."

Rick on Space and Time

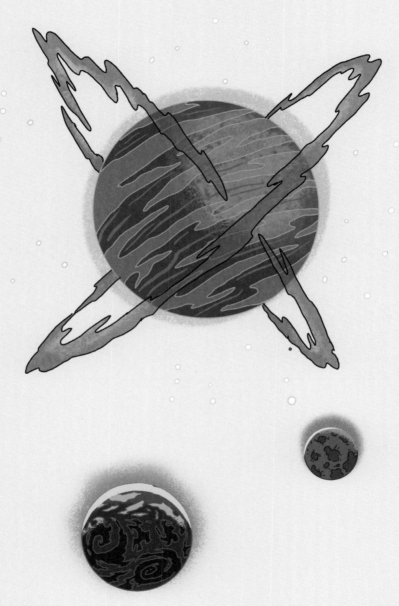

26

The World According to Rick

"By the way, life on other planets exists. Don't let it distract you."

Rick on Space and Time

"Imagine doing anything you want, then hopping to a timeline where you never did it. Imagine going anywhere, anytime, with nobody able to stop you."

The World According to Rick

"We'll keep saving the Earth, but not because it contains America. Because moving to a new version of Earth is a BLEEP and a half."

Rick on Space and Time

"You can alter anything you want about a totally fabricated origin story."

The World According to Rick

"Cosmic apotheosis wears off faster than salvia."

Rick on Memory and Reality

The World According to Rick

"Let's go, Morty. We've got a lot of friends and family to exterminate. We need to kill everyone that we can only remember fondly!"

Rick on Memory and Reality

"Don't break your back creating a lesson,
Morty. It's a free-form anthology.
I'm getting annoyed you're not hearing
that. As you can see around me, your
mind's been blown countless times,
and not always . . . by yourself."

The World According to Rick

"Nothing you think matters, matters.
This isn't special. This is happening infinite
times across infinite realities."

Rick on Memory and Reality

The World According to Rick

"Take a deep breath, and breathe that in. Breathe that fresh air in. You smell that? That's the smell of adventure, Morty."

Rick on Adventure

"Out of the frying pan, dot dot dot,
huh, Morty?"

The World According to Rick

"Simple and fun? Yeah, that's real easy to say from the sidekick position. But how about next time you be in charge, then we'll talk about how simple and fun it is."

40

The World According to Rick

"Let's make it interesting, Morty. If your adventure sucks, and we bail halfway through it, you lose the right to [BLEEP] about all future adventures. Plus, you have to do my laundry for a month."

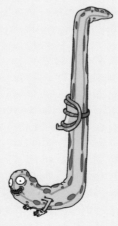

Rick on Adventure

"A good adventure needs a good ending."

The World According to Rick

"BLEEP Earth. You realize our planet's name means 'dirt,' right? We'll find a new world."

Rick on Adventure

44

The World According to Rick

"I refuse to answer a literal call to adventure, Morty. Let it go to voicemail."

Rick on Adventure

"Morty, I need your help on an adventure. Eh, 'need' is a strong word."

The World According to Rick

"Here's some things an adventure needs: conflict, stakes, a way for me to benefit, and, clearly, Morty."

Rick on Adventure

48   The World According to Rick

"Alright, Morty. [BLEEP] this noise. Let's get out of here and go on a classic Rick and Morty adventure."

Rick on Adventure

"Listen Morty, I hate to break it to you, but what people call 'love' is just a chemical reaction that compels animals to breed. It hits hard, Morty, then it slowly fades, leaving you stranded in a failing marriage. I did it, your parents are gonna do it. Break the cycle, Morty. Focus on science."

The World According to Rick

"It appears the lower tier of this society is being manipulated through sex and advanced technology by a hidden ruling class. Sound familiar?"

Rick on Love and Sex

The World According to Rick

"Listen, if this is an invasion, I
gotta sit this one out, but I'll be
back to have sex with the survivors."

Rick on Love and Sex

"The liver's under maintenance. Reuben's seen some rough years, Morty. Don't judge. You don't agree to have a theme park built inside you if your life's going great."

The World According to Rick

"If you'll excuse me, I've got pancakes back home with syrup on top of them, they're about to hit that critical point of syrup-absorption that turns the cakes into a gross paste, and I hate to get all Andy Rooney about it, but I think we all like fluffy discs of cake with syrup on top, and I think we also like to be accused of crimes when there's evidence. So, as they say in Canada, peace oot!"

Rick on Food and Drink

56

The World According to Rick

"Morty, if you go to where there's a bunch of ice cream and then you don't come back, you haven't actually gotten ice cream, you've just gone where ice cream is."

Rick on Food and Drink

"I'd like to get a ten-piece McNuggets, and a bunch of the Szechuan sauce. Like, as much as you're allowed to give me."

The World According to Rick

"I want that McNugget sauce, Morty.
That's my series arc, Morty.
If it takes nine seasons, I want my
Szechuan dipping sauce, Morty."

Rick on Food and Drink

"I just upgraded our cable package with programming from every conceivable reality."

The World According to Rick

"Who wants to watch random, crazy TV
shows from alternate dimensions,
and who wants to narcissistically obsess
about their alternate selves?"

Rick on Arts and/or Culture

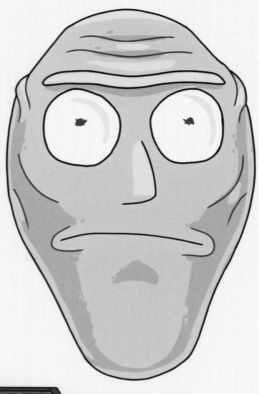

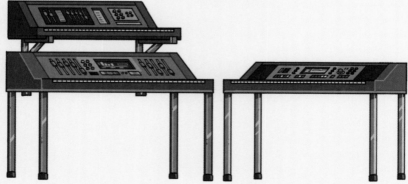

The World According to Rick

"Alright, Morty, let's do it. Why don't you find a button on one of those keyboards and lay down some kind of beat. Good music comes from people who are relaxed. Just hit a button, Morty! Give me a beat!"

Rick on Arts and/or Culture

"It's a prehistoric planet, Morty,
someone has to bring a little culture."

The World According to Rick

"So, you're mining stuff to craft with,
and crafting stuff to mine with.
Did your dad write this game?"

Rick on Arts and/or Culture

66

The World According to Rick

"Morty, you're bumming me out. Can't we just pretend like everything's fine for a few hours, enjoy ourselves, and then worry about all this later?"

Rick on Rest and Relaxation

67

"You're talking about taking over planets and galaxies. You gotta just remember to let go sometimes, you know?"

The World According to Rick

"Best weekend ever, Rick.
I agree, Rick."

Rick on Rest and Relaxation

The World According to Rick

"I don't want to overstep my bounds or anything. It's your house, it's your world, you're a real Julius Caesar. But I'll tell you how I feel about school. It's a waste of time. Bunch of people running around, bumping into each other. Guy up front says 'two plus two,' people in the back say 'four.' Then the bell rings and they give you a carton of milk and a piece of paper that says you can go take a dump or something. I mean it's, it's not a place for smart people."

Rick on Education

"School is stupid. It's not how you learn things. Morty is a gifted child, he has a special mind, that's why he's my little helper. He's like me, he's gonna be doing great science stuff later in his life. He's too smart for school. He needs to keep hanging out and helping me."

The World According to Rick

"Homework is stupid.
The whole point is to get less of it."

Rick on Education

The World According to Rick

"I probably could turn myself into a teenager and hang out in the zit-covered, hormone-addled, low stakes ass-world that is high school. But here's my reverse-ask: Why in the BLEEP would I ever do that, ever?"

The World According to Rick

"I'm sorry, Morty. It's a bummer. In reality, you're as dumb as they come."

Rick on Intelligence

"This must be the best day of your life.
You get to be the mayor of
I Told You Town. You're welcome."

The World According to Rick

"You're a perfect, impenetrable suit of human armor, Morty, because you're as DUMB as I am SMART. Which is why when I say shut up, it's really good advice."

Rick on Intelligence

The World According to Rick

"As you know, Morty, I've got a lot of enemies in the universe that consider my genius a threat: galactic terrorists, a few sub-galactic dictators, most of the entire intergalactic government. Wherever you find people with heads up their asses, someone wants a piece of your grandpa. And a lot of versions of me on different timelines had the same problem."

"Genius happens in the moment, Morty."

The World According to Rick

"That's planning for failure, Morty.
Even dumber than regular planning."

Rick on Intelligence

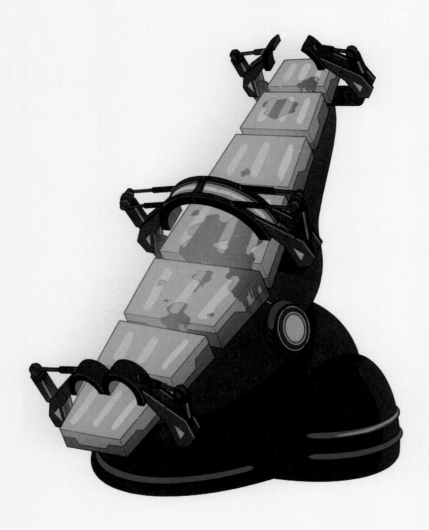

84

The World According to Rick

"OK, have fun in what's left of my brain. I'm gonna transfer to yours. Oh, there's not enough room for all my genius, so I'm leaving you with my fear of wicker furniture, my desire to play the trumpet, my tentative plans to purchase a hat, and six years of improv workshops. Comedy comes in threes."

Rick on Intelligence

"Everybody wants people they like to be right. That's why popular people are BLEEPing dumb. And why your pretentious, poorly written high-budget friends back there can eat a double-decker BLEEP sandwich."

The World According to Rick

"When you know nothing matters, the universe is yours, and I've never met a universe that was into it. The universe is basically an animal. It grazes on the ordinary. Creates infinite idiots just to eat them."

Rick on Intelligence

88

The World According to Rick

"That's clever, Morty, but I don't use color to sort things because I'm not a mouse in a European children's book."

Rick on Intelligence

"There is no god, Summer. Gotta rip that Band-Aid off now. You'll thank me later."

The World According to Rick

"Well, scientifically, traditions
are an idiot thing."

Rick on Tradition

92

The World According to Rick

"Weddings are basically funerals with cake. If I wanted to watch someone throw their life away, I'd hang out with Jerry all day."

Rick on Tradition

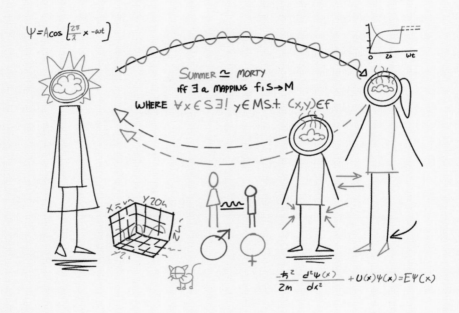

"Alright, listen, kids. No matter what happens to you, no matter what you do, Grandpa will always think of you both as high-maintenance, low-functioning, crybaby pieces of BLEEP . If there's a competition between the two of you, you're both tied for loser. You're equally terrible grandkids. I can mathematically prove it, too. Let me get my whiteboard. This has been a long time coming anyway."

Rick on Home and Family

"Listen. I'm not the nicest guy in the universe. Because I'm the smartest, and being nice is something stupid people do to hedge their bets. Now, I haven't been exactly subtle about how little I trust marriage. I couldn't make it work, and I can turn a black hole into a sun, so, at a certain point you've gotta ask yourself, what are the odds this is legit and not just some big lie we're all telling ourselves because we're afraid to die alone, because you know that's exactly how we all die. Alone."

The World According to Rick

"To friendship, to love, and to my
greatest adventure yet:
opening myself up to others!"

Rick on Home and Family

98

The World According to Rick

"You heard your mom, we've got adventures to go on, Morty. Just you and me, and sometimes your sister and sometimes your mom, but never your dad. You wanna know why, Morty? Because he crossed me. Oh, it gets darker, Morty. Welcome to the darkest year of our adventures. First thing that's different: no more dad, Morty. He threatened to turn me in to the government, so I made him and the government go away. I've replaced them both as the de facto patriarch of your family and your universe. Your mom wouldn't have accepted me if I came home without you and your sister, so now you know the real reason I rescued you. I just took over the family, Morty!

And if you tell your mom or sister I said any of this I'll deny it, and they'll take my side because I'm a hero, Morty. And now you're gonna have to go and do whatever I say, Morty! Forever!"

Rick on Home and Family

"Grandpa's concern for your
safety is fleeting!"

The World According to Rick

"There's no replacing either of you without an amount of work that would ultimately defeat the purpose."

Rick on Home and Family

The World According to Rick

"We don't really buy into that kind of crap. To the extent that love is an expression of familiarity over time, my access to infinite timelines precludes the necessity of attachment. In fact, I even abandoned one of my infinite daughters in an alternate version of Earth that was taken over by mutants."

Rick on Home and Family

"You're not gonna believe this
because it usually never happens,
but I made a mistake."

The World According to Rick

"C'mon Morty, luck had nothing
to do with it. I'm great.
That's the real reason."

Rick on Rick

The World According to Rick

"My brain is like a computer
the size of the sun."

Rick on Rick

"I've got an emo streak.
It's part of what makes me so rad."

The World According to Rick

"[BLEEP] it, I love myself"

Rick on Rick

The World According to Rick

"Guess who just discovered a new
element? Think you could do that,
Morty? You think anyone but me could
do that, ever, in a billion years?
The answer is no."

Rick on Rick

"I had all my problems removed. My entitlement, my narcissism, my crippling loneliness, my irrational attachments. They must be somewhere."

The World According to Rick

"You gotta have a sense of humor about these things. Oh, wait, you can't. You're literally incapable of seeing the bigger picture. I guess it's just funny because you've never done anything but complain about me being in charge, but if I ever gave you the wheel we'd be dead in five minutes."

Rick on Rick

The World According to Rick

"The world is full of idiots who don't understand what's important. And they'll tear us apart, Morty. But if you stick with me, I'm gonna accomplish great things, and you're gonna be part of them. And together we're gonna run around, Morty, and we're gonna do all kinds of wonderful things. Just you and me, Morty.

The outside world is our enemy. We're the only friends we've got, Morty. Just Rick and Morty and their adventures. Rick and Morty time, forever and forever. A hundred years, Rick and Morty's things. Me and Rick and Morty running around, and Rick and Morty time. All day long, forever."

Rick on Morty

"You're growing up fast, Morty.
You're growing into a real big
thorn straight up into my ass."

The World According to Rick

"When a Rick is with a Morty,
the genius waves get cancelled out
by the, uh, Morty waves."

Rick on Morty

117

The World According to Rick

"Why don't you make me, implausibly naive pubescent boy with an old Jewish comedy writer's name?"

Rick on Morty

119

"Excuse me, bartender. Can you make me a Dumb Grandson Pep Talk? It's one-part lame advice about stuff you know nothing about, and a lot of vodka."

"Don't worry, Morty, they love
you. Superheroes need a wide-eyed
unremarkable to take along and react
to everything like it's mind-blowing."

Rick on Morty

The World According to Rick

"You were a scary [BLEEP]ing kid, man. I didn't make Froopyland to get rid of you, Beth. I did it to protect the neighborhood. Not in a noble sense. It was just more practical to sequester you before I had to start, you know, cloning a replacement for every less-than-polite little boy or gullible animal that might cross your socio-path."

Rick on Beth

"Dude, bad father all the way to the max over here. I'm a [BLEEP]ing nutcase, and the acorn plopped straight down, baby. Look at some of this [BLEEP] you were asking me to make you as a kid: ray guns, a whip that forces people to like you, invisibility cuffs, a parent trap, a lightning gun, a teddy bear with anatomically correct innards, night vision googly-eye glasses, sound-erasing sneakers, false fingerprints, fall-asleep darts, a lie-detecting doll, an indestructible baseball bat, a taser shaped like a ladybug, a fake police badge, location-tracking stickers, rainbow-colored duct tape, mind-control hair clips, poison gum, and a pink, sentient switchblade."

The World According to Rick

"Beth, you know, when smart people get happy, they stop recognizing themselves. And you are very smart. Because you're very much my daughter."

Rick on Beth

125

The World According to Rick

"You're worse than evil,
Beth, you're smart."

Rick on Beth

128

The World According to Rick

"Not now, Jerry. I've got much, much smaller fish to fry."

Rick on Jerry

"Yeah, good one Jerry. 2003 just called. It wants its easy target back."

The World According to Rick

"No amount of genius can stop your dumb, mediocre, vacuous roots from digging into everything and everyone around you and draining them of any ability to fend you off."

Rick on Jerry

The World According to Rick

"Summer's just a hyper-emotional, needy little what-do-you-call-it . . . human. It runs in the family. I can tolerate it, but I can't give a BLEEP about it."

Rick on Summer

 134

The World According to Rick

"I don't do Adventures
with chicks, Summer."

Rick on Summer

135

"I don't like it here, Morty.
I can't abide bureaucracy. I don't
like being told where to go or what
to do. I consider it a violation."

The World According to Rick

"Don't hate the player,
hate the game, son."

Rick on Freedom

"Two things I want to make clear to everyone in this room: Never betray me, and it's time to go."

The World According to Rick

"I say, appreciate the life you have, because it can always be worse."

Rick on Freedom

The World According to Rick

"Right, yeah, like nothing shady ever happened in a fully-furnished office? You ever hear about Wall Street, Morty? You know what those guys do in their fancy board rooms? They take their balls and they dip them in cocaine and wipe them all over each other. You know, Grandpa goes around and he does his business in public because Grandpa isn't shady."

Rick on Crime and Punishment

"Yeah, sure, I mean, if you spend all day shuffling words around you can make anything sound bad, Morty."

The World According to Rick

"I'm sorry you think you
deserve an apology."

Rick on Crime and Punishment

The World According to Rick

"I wish I had this idea. Well, I did have this idea, but I wish I was the version of me that owned it. That guy's rich."

Rick on Money and Business

"Ugh, you've got what the intergalactic call a very planetary mindset, Morty. It's more complicated out here."

The World According to Rick

"The first rule of space travel, kids, is always check out distress beacons. Nine out of ten times it's a ship full of dead aliens and a bunch of free BLEEP!"

Rick on Money and Business

148

The World According to Rick

"Come on, this can't really be the way I go out. This is the mega-genius equivalent of dying on the toilet."

Rick on Death

"Morty, twenty people try to kill me every week. I end up getting high with half of them."

The World According to Rick

"Alright kid, I don't know much aside
from the fact that *Men in Black 2*
was a joyless cash grab, but I DO know
that whatever you have brewing around in
your noggin really connected with you.
I can't deny that, and I can't deny
that I'm inspired by your passion.
I want in. Suicide pact!"

Rick on Death

 152

The World According to Rick

"How is 'knocking out' a deterrent?
Everyone wants to be knocked out.
Nobody wants to be dead."

Rick on Death

"I'll be right back. I gotta take a family. That's my new word for poop."

The World According to Rick

"I know this is your world, not mine. The sooner I can get out, the sooner I can go back to taking big craps and you can go back to subsisting on them."

Rick on Toilet Talk

156

The World According to Rick

"That's Rick-diculous."

Rick on Catchphrases

157

"I have a new catchphrase. 'I love my grandkids.' Psych, just kidding! My new catchphrase is, 'I don't give a [BLEEP]!'"

The World According to Rick

"You have the right to kiss my BLEEP."

Rick on Catchphrases

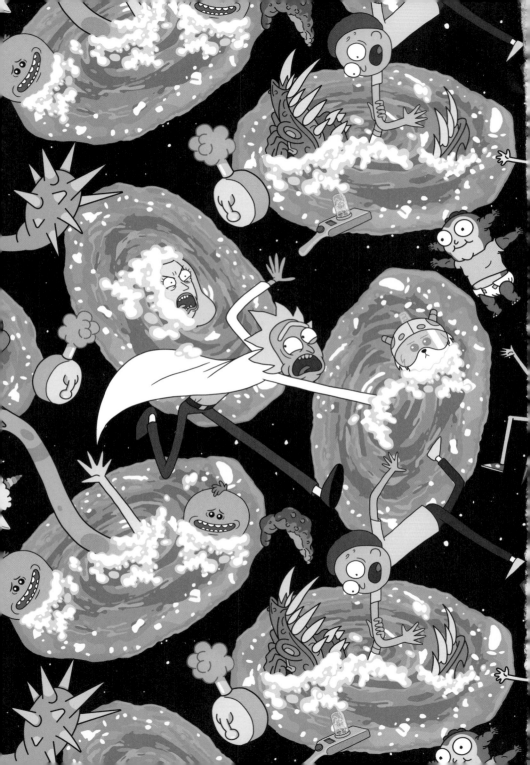